A Beginner's Guide to Fly Fishing

Table of Contents

A Beginner's Guide to Fly Fishing

According to written records, the art of fishing with an artificial fly actually dates all of the way back to the Romans! In fact, many credit the first recorded use of an artificial fly to the Roman author Claudius Aelianus near the end of the 2nd century C.E. since Claudius is the first to describe the practice of Macedonian anglers on the Astraeus River using flies made from red wool and cock feathers. Unfortunately, very little other material was written on the early history of fly fishing until *"The Treatyse on Fysshynge with an Angle"* which is attributed to author Dame Juliana Berners whose treatise was published in 1496 within The Boke of St. Albans. Fortunately for modern fly fishermen, technology has advanced far beyond that of Dame Berners' time and thus, modern fly anglers have access to both gear and knowledge that would be considered magical by both Roman's and early English anglers. Therefore, in the following guide, you will find all of the basic knowledge that you need to get started in this fascinating form of outdoor recreation such as the type of gear you need to enter the sport and how to find places to fly fish as well as an explanation of how to choose the right gear, an insight into Trout and their environment, a basic lesson in Trout foods and their imitations and last, information on approach, presentation, and short range fly casting technique.

Why You Should You Learn to Fly Fish -

While the reasons for learning to fly fish are as many and varied as fly fishermen themselves, the main reason that most people enter this sport is that fly fishing is an art form that requires an intimate knowledge of the fish species, their environment, and their preferred food sources and thus, it is a challenging and never ending learning experience that can keep an angler engaged for the entire course of his or her life. Also, the art of fly fishing differs drastically from any other form of fishing although, the various types of flies that fly fishermen use do tend to emulate other forms of fishing. For instance, drifting a nymph through the current with a fly rod is very similar to drifting a worm with a spinning rod and, stripping a streamer fly through a deep pool is very similar to retrieving a minnow or crayfish lure. However, the art of fishing on the surface with one of the many different types of dry flies is perhaps the most fascinating aspect of this sport since it is unlike any other type of fishing. In fact, there are fly anglers who have spent their entire lives perfecting their skills at this art and it's no wonder that they do so since there is simply no other thrill on the face of the planet that rivals the adrenalin rush you get when you make the perfect presentation to a prime lie and then see a huge trout rise from the depths to gulp your helpless May Fly or Caddis Fly imitation before it escapes! In fact, the art of fly fishing is really all about matching wits with one of the wiliest and wariest of fish species in existence and then fooling them into believing that our your artificial imitation is actually the real thing. But, it should also be noted that due to technological advances, fly fishing is a sport that is open to anglers of all incomes and all ages as well as all fish species. In fact, it has been proven that any fish species that will strike a lure will also strike a fly and thus, there are dedicated fly anglers who successfully pursue, Bass, Pike, Muskie, Sunfish, Carp, and even Catfish. Furthermore, fly fishing is not limited to freshwaters species and thus, fly anglers can choose to expand their horizons by perusing Stripers, Blues, Redfish, Bonefish, Permit, Tarpon, and even pelagic bluewater species such as Tuna, Sailfish, and Marlin. Therefore, no matter where you live, if there is water nearby that supports a fish population of any species, you too can become a fly fisherman. However, because fly fishing originated as a means of catching Trout, the following information will be focused on that species but, as you read through it, you should be aware all of the knowledge presented here can be applied to any fish species anywhere in the world.

What You Need to Get Started Fly Fishing -

Like any other type of fishing, fly fishing requires the fly angler to have certain gear such as a fly rod, a fly reel, a fly line, a fly leader and a collection of flies along with some accessories such as silicone past, nippers, strike indicators, hemostats, ect. Also, because casting a fly requires the same amount of room behind you as the distance you are attempting to cast to in front of you, fly fishermen often find it necessary stand in the middle of the stream and thus, if you intend to wade in cold water, both waders and wading boots are also necessities. However, you should also be aware that fly rods, fly reels, and fly lines are all purpose specific and thus, they are divided into those that are designed for freshwater use and those that are designed for saltwater use with some overlap depending on species. In addition, you should also be aware that casting a fly differs drastically from casting a lure or bait in that a fly has very little weight and a lot of wind resistance and thus, rather than depending on the weight of the fly to bend the rod (called loading) and thus store and then release the energy needed to propel the fly, fly fishermen instead use a weighted line. Therefore, all fly lines have a numerical designation that corresponds to the weight of the first thirty feet of the line weighed in grains (440 grains equals one ounce). Thus, fly lines range from 1 weight to 14 weight with one being the lightest and

14 being the heaviest (this also relates to tensile strength). Consequently, the larger the fly, the heavier the fly line that is required to cast it due to its wind resistance and thus, fly rods are also designated according to both the weight of fly line that they are designed to cast as well as their length. For instance, freshwater fly rods range from 1 wt. to 6 wt. and saltwater rods range from 6 wt. to 14 wt. However, they also differ in length from as little as six feet to as much as 14 feet depending on their intended use. But, the most popular freshwater fly rod is the 9 ft. 5 wt. and the most popular saltwater fly rod is the 9 ft. 9 wt. with those shorter or longer or, those designed to cast lighter or heavier fly lines, being chosen for specific purposes such as fishing for Trout on small streams, fishing for Salmon or Steelhead on large rivers, or fishing for large saltwater species such as Tarpon.

Therefore, use the following guidelines to choose an appropriate fly rod, fly reel, and fly line outfit for the particular type of fly fishing you intend to pursue:

1 – 2 weight lines	Ultralight	Excellent for delicate dry fly presentation toskittish fish in crystal clear water.
3-4 weight lines	Light	Best for general purpose presentation to trout with small flies at short to medium ranges.

5-6 weight lines	Medium	Best weights for general purpose, freshwater use and
	Light	especially for long distances or casting large flies.
7-8 weight lines	Medium	Excellent for small to medium saltwater species.
	Heavy	
9-10 weight lines	Heavy	Excellent for strong wind or casting large flies over long distances and for large saltwater species.
11-14 weight lines	Big Game	Designed for big-game saltwater species such as Tarpon, Sail Fish, Sword Fish, ect.

Of course, in addition to an appropriate fly rod, you will also need an appropriate fly line and thus, you should also be aware that modern fly lines are available in a myriad of different specialty tapers in addition the many different weights. For instance, freshwater fly lines are available in either Double Taper or Weight Forward designs and each has its advantages and disadvantages.

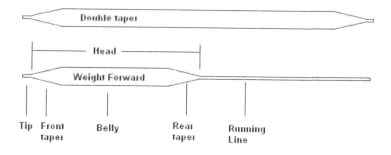

line taper diagram

For instance, Double Tapers are often easier to cast than Weight Forward tapers but, they will not cast as far. Also, if one end of a Double Taper becomes damaged, you can simply remove it from the fly reel and turn it around which you cannot do with a Weight Forward taper. On the other hand, all of the specialty tapers available today are Weight Forward tapers such those designed for extra delicate presentation or those designed specifically for casting large flies or those designed for casting long distances. Furthermore, you should also be aware that some fly lines are designed to float on the surface of the water while other are designed to sink beneath the surface at different rates of speed to enable fly anglers to reach fish species that do not normally feed on the surface. Plus, there are hybrid lines that have a body that floats on the surface with a tip that is designed to sink that are especially useful for fishing with streamer flies. Therefore, the weight of the fly line that you choose will depend on range fly sizes of the fly you intend to cast and the taper that you choose will depend on the particular fish species you intend to pursue.

Fly Size vs. Fly Line Weight

(Fly Size)

Fly Line Weight	6/0	5/0	4/0	3/0	2/0	1/0	2	4	6	8	10	12	14	16	18	20	22	24	26	28
1													X	X	X	X	X	X	X	X
2												X	X	X	X	X	X	X	X	X
3											X	X	X	X	X	X	X			
4										X	X	X	X	X	X	X				
5									X	X	X	X	X	X	X					
6								X	X	X	X	X	X	X						
7							X	X	X	X	X	X	X							
8						X	X	X	X	X	X	X								
9					X	X	X	X	X	X	X									
10			X	X	X	X	X													
11	X	X	X	X	X															

Then, once you have chosen an appropriate fly rod and fly line, you will need an appropriate fly reel to mate with your fly rod to store and contain your fly line. Therefore, just like fly rods, fly reels are also divided into those intended for freshwater use and those intended for saltwater use although this distinction is far less clear than with fly rods. However, the main differences are size, weight, and the size of the arbor (the post in the center of the fly reel). For instance, fly reels are available in small, medium, and large sizes and with standard, mid, and large arbors. Also, as a general rule, all small fly reels have standard arbors and are intended for freshwater use whereas medium sized fly reels can have either standard or mid-arbors and are designed for either freshwater or saltwater use whereas, large fly reels almost always have large arbors and are almost always designed for saltwater use. Plus, in addition to the fly line, all fly reels are designed to carry a certain length of thin, Dacron, line called "backing" which greatly extends the amount of distance that an fly angler can allow the fish to run since most fly lines are only 90 feet in length. Thus, the smaller the reel, the less backing it can hold and the large the fly reel, the more backing it can hold. In addition, it should be noted that fly reels with standard arbors have the slowest rate of retrieve whereas a large arbor fly reels have the highest rate of retrieve with mid-arbors falling in between. Thus, most trout fishermen prefer small, lightweight, fly reels with either standard or mid-arbors and most saltwater fly fishermen favor large fly reels with large arbors. Furthermore, fly reels are available with either spring-and-pawl drag systems or disc drag systems and the particular fish species that you choose to pursue will also determine which drag system you need since large fish species require more stopping power than small fish species.

Thus, while small stream Trout fishermen can get by with a spring-and-pawl drag, larger Trout and lager fish species will require a disc drag.

However, because fly lines are necessarily large in diameter due to their weighted coating, it is physically impossible to tie a fly onto the end of your fly line and, even if you could, you would not want to because the fly line is highly visible to the fish. Therefore, a tapered fly leader is instead attached to the end of the fly line via a loop connector or nail knot and then the fly is attached to the end of the small end of the leader. Also, it should be noted that fly leaders come in three different types consisting of extruded leaders (the most common type), knotted leaders (older technology) and braided leaders (the oldest technology) as well as different lengths and different tippet diameters and each leader is designated by its length and tippet diameter (the small end of the leader). Furthermore, it should be noted that the larger the fly, the stiffer the leader required to cast it and thus, small flies can be cast with small diameter tippets but, large flies must be cast with large diameter tippets.

What length and size leader should you use?

Leader Length Chart

Leader Length	Best suited for...
6 foot	Sinking fly lines of all types, sunfish, bass, trout in tiny, brushy streams.
7.5 foot	Trout in streams from 10-20 feet wide, intermediate and sinking tip lines in lakes and saltwater conditions where the fish are not terribly spooky. Also streamer fishing for trout with big flies or with heavy nymphs and big indicators
9 foot	Trout streams larger than 20 feet wide where the water is mostly riffled, or else the fish are not spooky. In salt water when the fish are in shallow water under bright, clear conditions.
12 foot	Trout in most lakes with floating lines. Trout in streams with flies smaller than size 16 when the water is flat, low, or very clear.
15 foot	Spooky trout in extremely clear water in both lakes and rivers.

Leader Size Chart

Tippet Size	Tippet Diameter	Approximate breaking strength in pounds	Balances with fly sizes:
8X	.003"	1.75	22, 24, 26, 28
7X	.004"	2.5	18, 20, 22, 24
6X	.005"	3.5	16, 18, 20, 22
5X	.006"	4.75	14, 16, 18
4X	.007"	6	12, 14, 16
3X	.008"	8.5	6, 8, 10
2X	.009"	11.5	4, 6, 8
1X	.010"	13.5	2, 4, 6
0X	.011"	15.5	1/0, 2, 4
.012	.012"	18.5	5/0, 4/0, 3/0, 2/0
.013	.013"	20	5/0, 4/0, 3/0, 2/0
.015	.015"	25	5/0, 4/0, 3/0, 2/0

Last, in addition to all of the other gear a fly fisherman has to have, there are numerous small items and gadgets that are also essential to the sport and a way to properly organize them is a must have item. Fortunately for us, a famous fly fisherman named Lee Wulff invented the fly vest as a way to organize and store all of your fly fishing paraphernalia. Thus, below you will find a list of the items you will need to carry in your fly vest divided into two categories consisting of items that you absolutely cannot do without and other items that are nice to have along but are not absolutely necessary.

Must Have Vest Items	Useful Vest Items

Fly Assortments-
    Dries
    Terrestrials
    Wets
    Nymphs
    Streamers
	Hat
	Sunglasses with *lightly* tinted,
	    polarized, lenses.
	Sun block
	
	Waterproof Digital Camera

Nylon Leaders
    4x, 5x
Nylon Tippet Material
    4x, 5x
Fluorocarbon Leaders
    2x, 3x, 4x
Fluorocarbon Tippet Material
    2x, 3x, 4x
	Toilet Paper
	
	Whistle
	Flashlight
	Extra Batteries
	First Aid kit
	Emergency rain poncho
	Space Blanket
	Waterproof matches

Fly Floatant Fly Sink (wetting agent) Nippers Hemostats	Fire Starter
Stream Thermometer Retractable Ruler Dry Fly Desiccant Strike indicators Mini split-shot Assortment Sink-tip System	

Fly Fishing Knots -

If you read any beginner's guide to fly fishing, you will inevitably encounter a chapter on fly fishing knots. Then, upon reading said chapter, you will be confronted with five different knots of increasing difficulty ending with the infamous Blood Knot which was distinctly designed to confound human anatomy since it requires four hands (or a jig) to tie this tricky knot. But, fear not because there are really only four different knots that you really need to know about and you will only use two of them once but, you will use the other two frequently.

But, before we examine of how to tie each knot, you first need to be aware of what each knot is used for. So, to start with, the Arbor Knot is used to fasten your Dacron backing to the arbor of your fly reel's spool and thus, you may only use it once or twice in all of the years you fly fish. If fact, the same could be said for the Nail Knot since it is used to fasten the Dacron backing to the end of your fly line and in some cases, to fasten a length of heavy monofilament with a loop to the other end of your fly line or possibly even for fastening the butt of your leader to the fly line. However, a much more elegant solution to this is to use a braided loop connector and then tie a Perfection Loop in the butt of your leader so that you can make a loop-to-loop connection. Then, of course, you will need to learn to tie the Clinch Knot to fasten your flies to the tippet end of your leader.

The Arbor Knot –

The "Arbor Knot" is a very simple knot that is used to attach the fly line backing to the arbor of the fly reel. However, even though it is the first knot used in the fly line backing to fly line to fly leader system, it is probably the least used knot of all fly fishing knots because most fly fishermen will only have a need for it once or twice in their entire careers as fly fishermen.

To tie this knot, loop the fly line backing around the arbor of the fly reel, then tie a simple overhand knot around the fly line backing. Then, tie another overhand knot just above the first knot (see illustration). Then, grasp the fly line backing behind the first knot you tied and pull it until the second knot abuts the first knot. Thus, locking it in place.

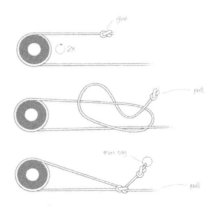

Arbor Knot Diagram

The Nail Knot -

The "Nail Knot" and the "Nailless Nail Knot" are used to attach the fly line backing to the fly line and to attach the fly line to the leader butt. However, like the Arbor Knot, the Nail Knot is one of the least often used fly fishing knots because it is hard to tie and, when used to attach a fly leader to a fly line, it makes changing leaders on the stream very difficult. Thus most experienced fly fishermen use a Braided Loop Connector instead.

Step 1.

However, to tie a Nail Knot, position a nail or similar item between the fly line and the fly leader. Next, loosely wrap the butt of the leader around the fly line fly line 5 to 8 times. (See illustration

Step 2.

Next, pass the end of the fly leader back through the loops you just created around the fly line. Then, grasp both the end of the fly leader and the fly line simultaneously and pull on both ends at the same time to tighten the knot. Then, carefully remove the nail.

Step 3.

Last, moisten the knot with saliva and again grasp both the end of the fly line and the end of the leader at the same time and finish tightening the knot. Last, clip off the excess line and fly leader close to the finished knot.

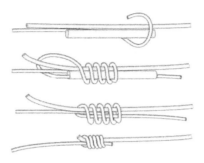

Nail Knot Diagram

The Perfection Loop –

The Perfection Loop is used any time you need to form a loop in monofilament line. For instance, you can use a Blood Knot to secure a length of monofilament to the end of your fly line and then tie a Perfection Loop in the end of the monofilament to form a loop to connect your leader to. In addition, a Perfection Loop is sometimes tied at the end of the fly leader just above the tippet section and then, a matching Perfection Loop is tied in the tippet and used to attach the leader to the tippet resulting in an easy to change, "loop-to-loop" connection.

Step 1

Hold the leader in your left hand and the tag end in your right hand and form a large loop. Also, make sure that the tag end of the leader is behind the standing end of the leader. Then, pinch the point where the two ends cross.

Step 2

Next, using the tag end, form a second, smaller, loop in front of the first loop and again pinch the point where the two cross.

Step 3

Next, pass the tag end between the two loops while continuing to pinch the point where the two loops cross.

Step 4

Next, reach through the large loop from behind and grasp the small loop.

Step 5

Last, pull the small loop through the big loop to tighten the knot while continuing to pinch the point where the two loops cross.

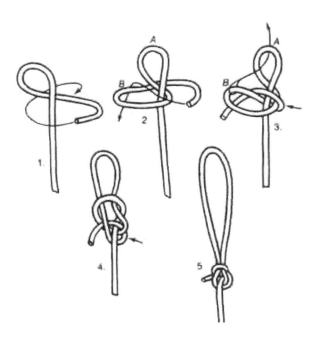

Perfection Loop diagram

The Clinch Knot –

As a fly fisherman, regardless whether you use the Clinch Knot or the Improved Clinch Knot, you will use this knot more often than any other fly fishing knot because it is the knot that is used for attaching the tippet to the fly.

Step 1

First, pass the end of the leader through the eye of the hook and wrap the leader around itself exactly five times (research has shown that five turns creates the strongest knot).

Step 2

Second, thread the end of the leader through the small loop above the eye and then, back through the big loop.

Step 3

Last, grasp the leader and the fly and pull the coils tight against the eye of the hook.

Step 4

Last, clip off the tag end of the leader

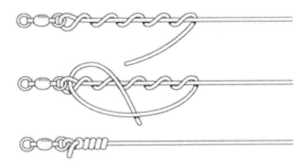

Clinch Knot diagram

How to Find Places to Fly Fish -

Of course, a major concern when contemplating entering the sport of fly fishing is where to fish and what species of fish to fish for. However, regardless of where you live, as long as there is a body of water nearby that contains fish, you can fly fish for them. But, because most people associate fly fishing with Trout, this section will focus on the different types of Trout water. Therefore, it is important to note that all Trout streams can be categorized as one of four different types of water: a Spring Creek, a Freestone Stream, a Limestone Stream, or a Tailwater and the definition of each type of stream is listed below:

Spring Creeks-

A Spring Creek is a stream who's *main source of water* is derived from ***rainfall resulting in <u>ground water accumulation</u>*** and which has a relatively constant temperature. Therefore, all mountain creeks are properly classified as Spring Creeks. In addition, many Spring Creeks originate in mountain ranges that have extensive deposits of limestone which is much softer than the surrounding granite rock. Thus, because the limestone erodes more easily than the harder rock, this erosion creates an extensive system of underground, mineral rich, creek, rivers, and reservoirs. When this mineral rich water emerges above ground as a spring and starts its journey downhill, it collects to form a Spring Creek or a Limestone Stream which in turn creates an exceptionally rich environment for aquatic plants, aquatic insects, and trout. Therefore, because both the water temperature and the volume of water in a Spring Creek is less erratic than that of a Freestone Stream and, because of the greater abundance of aquatic plants and aquatic insects, fish inhabiting a Spring Creek are generally larger than those inhabiting a Freestone Stream because they have a longer growing season and more food available to them.

Limestone Streams-

Limestone Streams are Spring Creeks that flow through large deposits of limestone either below and/or above ground and are most often associated with streams that have a relatively consistent water temperature and a relatively consistent and relatively slow current. Therefore, the phrase "Limestone Stream" is most often associated with streams that have a low gradient and a gentle current along with extensive beds of aquatic plants which in turn create an exceptionally rich environment for various species of aquatic insects and the trout that feed on them. Consequently, Limestone Streams are the richest environment available to trout because of the profuse, abundance of food, the lack of a swift current, and the lack of extreme temperatures. Thus, fish inhabiting Limestone Streams are often notably larger than fish inhabiting any of other three types of streams. However, although their topography differs greatly from the aforementioned definition, many Spring Creeks are also Limestone Streams because they too flow through large deposits of limestone.

Freestone Streams-

A Freestone Stream is a stream from which *main source of water* is derived from **_runoff_ created by either melting snow or rainfall**. They are characterized by drastically fluctuating water levels, steep gradients, and rapids during periods of high water flow. Therefore, because the supply of water in a Freestone Stream is so erratic, the volume of water in a Freestone Stream tends to peak during the early summer months and tends to diminish during the late fall and winter months and thus, a Freestone Stream is more readily influenced by the ambient air temperature. In turn, this results in a wider range of water temperatures than those of either Spring Creeks or Limestone Streams and thus winter can cause Freestone Streams to reach near freezing temperatures and summer can cause them to rise to temperatures as high as 70* F (which is the extreme upper limit of the temperature range within which trout can survive). Therefore, because the wide variation in both water volume and water temperature, coupled with the lack of dissolved minerals in a Freestone Stream, a Trout's growing season (which occurs at water temperatures between 45° - 65°F) is drastically shortened. Consequently, the fish that inhabit Freestone Streams are generally notably smaller than those that inhabit Spring Creeks, Limestone Streams, or Tailwaters.

Tail Waters-

Tail Waters are streams that are located below a dam which contains a reservoir and from which water is expelled from the bottom of the dam. Since this expelled water is drawn from the bottom of the reservoir, it has a consistently cold temperature which provides an excellent environment for various species of aquatic plants, aquatic insects, and trout for a couple of miles downstream of the dam. Consequently, most Tail Waters provide a rich environment for trout because they remain at a relatively constant temperature throughout the year and, they tend to produce *very* prolific insect hatches along with providing an extended growing season for trout. Therefore, trout inhabiting Tail Waters can easily be as large and as numerous as those inhabiting Limestone Streams and both the terrain and the current are often much less rugged than that of a Spring Creek or a Freestone Stream.

Furthermore, finding these bodies of water is as easy as looking at a topographical map such as a DeLorme Gazetteer for your state. When doing so, all ponds, lakes, creeks, streams, and rivers will be shown in blue and any roads leading to them will also be shown. Also, a quick perusal of a U.S. Geological Survey map displaying mineral deposits is an excellent way to locate Limestone and/or Spring Creeks. Therefore, lack of a place to fly fish is no longer an excuse for procrastinating!

Understanding Trout and Their Environment -

"In order to do, we must first understand what it is we are doing." Therefore, understanding the environment that Trout inhabit is essential to learning how to fly fish for them. Consequently, you must first understand that from the day a Trout is born as an egg to day it dies, there are aquatic, terrestrial, and avian predators that are looking to make a meal of it. Thus, if a Trout is to survive, it necessarily becomes *very* paranoid! As a result, all Trout seem to adopt an attitude of "If it moves, RUN! If it doesn't move, RUN ANYWAY!" Thus, if a trout sees any movement whatsoever within its cone of vision, its first instinct is to dart into the nearest Sheltering Lie and stay there until he feels like the threat has passed. So, as a fly fisherman, it is absolutely imperative that you learn to become very stealthy in your approach to a prospective trout lie. In fact, when fly fishing for trout, it is helpful to adopt the attitude of a hunter rather than that of the average fisherman. Therefore, you should take advantage of any available cover to hide your approach to a prospective trout lie such as moving along the bank where your are hidden by trees instead of wading up center of the stream, hiding behind boulders, or crouching down so that you are below the trout's cone of vision.

How a Trout Sees His World -

Although understanding how a fish thinks is paramount to enabling you to catch fish, it is also important to understand how they see their world. Thus, the following description applies to all fish species in any type of water but, this section will focus specially on Trout.

Thus, if you were a Trout lying on the bottom of a stream, if you were to look up, you would see a huge mirror hanging over your head and that mirror would reflect an exact replica of the stream bed and anything located beneath the surface of the water. However, you would also see a round hole in this mirror located directly above your eyes that would provide you with a limited vision of the world above the surface of the water and, the cause of this phenomenon is a law of physics called Snell's Law that states *"any light waves striking the surface of water at an angle that is greater than 45° will enter the water and, any light waves striking the surface of water at an angle that is less than 45° will be reflected"*. But, unless you are holding in perfectly still water, the image of the surface world you see through this window would be distorted by the current and any ripples caused by riffles, runs, or rapids. Thus, if you were holding in white water (as Rainbow Trout often do), then instead of seeing an image of the surface world, you would instead see a white froth of air bubbles and distortions caused by the current. In addition, the size of the hole through with you see the surface world would depend on the depth at which you were holding because, the diameter of the hole through which you can see is two-and-one-quarter times the depth at which you are holding. Therefore, if you were holding at a depth of two feet, then you would have a round window over your head approximately four and one half feet in diameter through which you could see the surface world. In addition, because the shape of this hole extends at a 45° angle from either side of the trout's eye (with the apex of the angle being located at the tout's eye), trout have 90 degrees of *vertical* vision under the water's surface. However, once the edge of this angle reaches the water's surface, it descends to a 10 degree angle. Consequently, trout actually have 160 degrees of vertical vision which is shaped like a cone extending upward from their eyes and thus, we call this their "Cone of Vision". Therefore, a fly fisherman approaching a potential trout lie will only have a 10 degree angle from the surface of the water in which to approach the trout unseen!

However, it is important to keep in mind that since this is an *angle*, it widens accordingly the further the apex is from the water's surface and narrows accordingly the closer the apex is to the water's surface. Therefore, the closer to the surface that a trout is holding, the smaller his cone of vision will be and the deeper he is holding, the wider his cone of vision will be. Also, the farther you are away from where a trout is holding, the less likely it is that he will see you and conversely, the closer you get, the more likely it is that he will see you. Thus, the average fly fisherman of average height wading in water that is approximately waist deep will only be able to approach a potential trout lie to within about fifteen feet without being seen and even less if you walking along the bank even with, or above, the water's surface. So, if you feel the need to approach the trout's lie any closer than this, you will need to crouch down closer to the water's surface or, use any available cover such as rocks or boulders to hide your approach. In addition, it is also important to keep in mind that trout have 330° of *horizontal* vision beneath the surface of the water which leaves a 30° blind spot directly behind them. Thus, since trout are anatomically designed to face upstream into the current, it is always best to approach a potential trout lie from downstream so that you approach them within their blind spot.

Last, while trout do have rudimentary ears and thus, they can hear some sound beneath the water's surface, they have a far more sensitive organ called the "Lateral Line" which extends the length of their body from head to tail that consists of a group of highly sensitive nerves that enables them to feel or "see" pressure waves in the water. Thus, when you are wading in the water and approaching a potential trout lie, it is imperative that you do so in as stealthy a manner as possible and as slowly as possible in order to minimize the pressure waves crated by your body moving through the water.

Consequently, approaching a wild trout in its natural environment without being seen or felt is a daunting task at best and one that takes years of practice to perfect. Therefore, anyone who is able to approach a wild Trout, then cast their fly precisely enough to land it within the trout's "cone of vision", and then cause that fly to drift in a way that looks entirely natural and thus entices the trout to take the fly, has accomplished a phenomenal feat of planning and stealthy execution of which they should be extremely proud regardless of the size of the trout they catch!

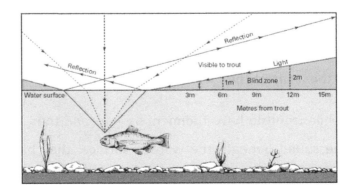

Cone of vision diagram

34

The Food vs. Energy Equation -

Furthermore, you should also be aware that trout are first born as an egg and then, as they mature, they grow through different stages based upon their size called Alevin, Fry, Fingerlings, Parr, and Juveniles before becoming sexually mature and thus being classified as Adults. Consequently, once a trout completes the Alevin stage by completely consuming its yoke sack, the only two things on its mind are avoiding predators and finding and consuming enough food to grow larger.

Consequently, all trout look for quite spots in the stream called "lies" where they can escape the constant pull of the current and yet have easy access to food without unduly exposing themselves to danger from predators. Therefore, such places as eddies located behind rock or a log adjacent to good current flow make excellent "prime lies". In addition, it is important to learn to identify prime lies because you will *always* find the largest trout in the prime lies. But, the reason for this is a concept called the "food vs. energy equation" which states that, in order for a trout to grow larger, it must gain more energy from the food it consumes than it expends in pursuing and capturing that food. Thus, it is helpful to think of the stream as a floating restaurant and the various aquatic and terrestrial insects drifting in the current as the menu and a trout's "prime lies" and "feeding lies" as their seat in the restaurant. So, when a tasty looking insect comes drifting downstream toward a trout's prime lie or feeding lie, all a trout has to do is decide whether or not he wants to dart out into the current and capture that insect. However, it is important to be aware that there are also numerous bits of organic debris drifting in the current along with all those tasty insects and thus, a trout must become very adept at discriminating what is actually edible from what is not edible and they learn to do this by learning to identify the size, shape, and color of the available insect species that inhabit or fall into their particular stream. In addition, they also look for signs of movement such as the gills located along the abdomen of May Fly and Damsel nymphs as an indicator of life because any trout that mistakenly captures non-edible food is wasting energy. Plus, any trout that spends time swimming in the current to capture food is also wasting energy unless there is a *tremendous* amount of food drifting in the current such as when a May Fly hatch is occurring. Thus, when such hatches do occur, trout will often leave their sheltered prime lies and hold in the center of the water column in the middle or tail of a pool in Feeding Lies in order to more easily capture these nymphs and the emerging Duns. But, this exposed position also makes them far more vulnerable to avian predators and thus, they are often very skittish when they are in feeding lies. However, the overabundance of food drifting in the current often makes the extra risk well worth the danger.

Now, in addition to the various species of aquatic and terrestrial insects drifting the current, there are also numerous species of small fish inhabiting the stream along with the adult trout such as Dace, Sculpins, and Chubs, and Crayfish along with trout in the various stages of maturity, and all of them are fair game as far as adult trout are concerned. Thus, I like to think of these various bait fish in this manner: if someone were to offer you your choice between a free McDonald's cheeseburger and a free 20 oz. steak dinner, which one would you choose? Personally, I would choose the steak dinner and most adult trout seem to feel the same way. So, although it obviously requires more energy to run down and capture a bait fish than it does a May Fly Dun, that baitfish provides FAR more energy than consuming a couple of nymphs mature adults. Therefore, trout will *almost always consume the largest meal available* as long as it provides them with more energy than they expend capturing that piece of food. Consequently, **larger flies tend to catch larger trout**.

But, it is also important to understand that when there is an overabundance of nymphs and duns drifting in the current such during a hatch, then trout will often become very selective in what they choose to eat for the duration of that hatch. Thus, they will often ignore any food item that is not the same size, shape, and color of the hatching insects because they have already determined through sampling that a particular insect is an edible source of food and thus it satisfies the food vs. energy equation.

The Three Types of Trout Lies -

As I mentioned in "The Food vs. Energy Equation" section, trout live in a constantly moving environment and thus, in order to conserve energy, they look for places in the stream that provide them with shelter from the current and these places area called "trout lies". However, as a fly fisherman, it is important that you understand that there are three different types of trout lies and each one serves a different purpose to the trout.

For instance, trout need places that they can run to for shelter whenever they feel threatened either from above or from below and we call these places "Sheltering Lies". Therefore, any trout that exists in given stream has undoubtedly thoroughly explored that section of the stream and thus, they know exactly where any nooks, crannies, ledges, and undercuts are that they can squeeze into deep enough to escape any predator that may be pursuing them. In addition, their instinct tells them that if they see any movement at all through that magical hole in the mirror above them that we call the "cone of vision" that might represent a danger to them, then their unconscious reaction is to dart for the nearest Sheltering Lie as fast as possible and stay there until they are certain the danger has passed. Therefore, a Sheltering Lie is defined as a place that provides a trout with shelter from predators but does not offer access to food. Consequently, good examples of Sheltering Lies are under or between large rocks, deep into the dark caves created by overhanging ledges, or beneath undercut stream banks.

On the opposite end of the scale, there are places in the stream where trout will gather during times when one species or another of aquatic insects are hatching even though it exposes them to predators and these places are called "Feeding Lies". However, these Feeding Lies are often chosen specifically because they require the trout to either expend very little energy to maintain their position in the current or, because that particular position concentrates the stream of hatching insects so that the tout can eat more of them while expending less energy. Consequently, these Feeding Lies most often occur in calm pools and glides where the water is crystal clear and the trout can suspended above the stream bed or in the shallow tail of a pool. Therefore, a Feeding Lie is a place where trout congregate *only* because it provides them easy access to an overabundance of drifting aquatic insects but, does not provide them with shelter from predators.

Last, there is a third category of Trout Lies that is the ultimate place in the stream for a trout to hold because it offers the trout both shelter from predators *and* easy access to food and these types of lies are called "Prime Lies". Consequently, no matter what stream, creek, or river you fish on, you will *always* find the largest fish in the Prime Lies simply because the Prime Lies are the best real estate available in that section of water and the largest, most aggressive, trout will always displace the smaller trout in the Prime Lie for that reason. After all, look at Japanese Sumo wrestlers; the ones who eat the most get the biggest, and the biggest Sumo wrestler is the one that usually manages to toss the opposing wrestler out of the ring.

Therefore, the way to identify a Prime Lie is to first look for places in the stream that would offer a trout shelter such an eddy behind a large rock, an eddy behind a log protruding into the stream or laying on the streambed either adjacent to or in the main current, or a ledge with a deep cave that faces upstream so that the trout can see any food items drifting toward it without exposing itself to danger. Also, the eddies on the edges of riffles and runs are also Prime Lies because the turbulent surface of the water makes it nearly impossible for predators to see the trout even in shallow water. In addition, the small pockets found in "Pocket Water" are excellent Prime Lies because the turbulent water around them sweeps a lot of food into the pockets. Last, water deeper than four feet (even if it is crystal clear) usually causes a trout feel reasonably safe and thus, they will often cruise in deeper water while rooting for nymphs or plucking Periwinkles.

So, now that you know about the three types of Trout Lies, the next time you approach your favorite trout stream, try approaching slowly while using the intervening foliage to conceal your presence and take some time to see if you notice trout congregating in the tails of the pools or cruising in the pools or glides and, if not, then proceed to approach and cast your fly *only* to the Prime Lies because everything else will either be barren water or hold only small trout.

The Different Types of Trout Flies -

The types of flies that fly fishermen use can be divided into several different categories and each category has its appropriate time and place. However, as a general rule of thumb, dry flies are the most exciting pattern to fish, nymphs tend to catch the most fish, and streamers tend to catch the largest fish. Now, the reason that dry flies are so exciting to fish is that when you are fishing on the surface, you can often see the fish rising to the surface to take the fly but, you have to set the hook *very* quickly or the fish will reject the fly. Nymphs, on the other hand, are often the most productive category of fly to fish with because trout often obtain the majority of their food from the sub-surface drift because it requires less energy and presents less danger than rising to the surface. Last, once a trout reaches maturity, it often becomes very difficult for them to obtain enough food from the drift and thus, they often turn to larger prey to satisfy their energy requirements. Therefore, streamers tend to attract the largest fish because they imitate forage fish such as Sculpins and Dace and crustaceans such as Crayfish.

Nymphs -

Nymph patterns are fished sub-surface on or near the bottom and are generally designed to represent May fly or Stone fly nymphs but, there are also some good, free-living and cased, Caddis fly larva imitations as well as some good Hellgrammite (Dobson Fly) imitations. Also, May Fly nymph patterns are designed to imitate immature May Flies that have accidently become dislodged from the rocks and gravel on the stream bed or nymphs that are rising to the surface to hatch. Whereas, Stone Fly nymph patterns are designed to imitate immature Stone Flies that have become dislodged from the rocks and gravel on the streambed and are tumbling in the current. Last, Hellgrammite patterns (aka "Grampers"), are designed to imitate the larval stage of the Dobson fly and are very aggressive predators of other aquatic insects. Thus, they are very mobile in the current and have large and powerful mandibles that can deliver a painful bite to both their pray and humans but, despite their ferocity, they are a favorite food of both Trout and Smallmouth Bass.

Larvae -

Larvae patterns are also fished sub-surface on or near the bottom and are generally designed to represent either free living or cased Caddis Fly larva that have accidently become dislodged from the rocks and gravel on the stream bed

Dry Flies -

Dry flies are fished on the surface of the water and are

generally designed to imitate either adult, adolescent, May flies or Caddis flies. Furthermore, Mayfly imitations are divided into two sub-categories called: Duns and Spinners whereas, a Dun imitates a mature *adolescent* May Fly that has just hatched and crawled out onto the surface of the water to let its wings dry before flying to the streamside foliage to complete the next stage of its life and a Spinner imitates a mature, *adult,* female, Mayfly that has returned to the water to lay her eggs and then died while over the water after having completed her lifecycle. Looking deeper into the May fly's life cycle, we see that they are born as eggs laid on the streambed which then hatch into nymphs that inhabit the steam bead for one to four years (depending on the species) before hatching into duns. Then, when the nymph is ready to hatch, it inflates its exoskeleton with air and rises to the surface where it suspends itself in the surface film. Once there, it splits open is carapace and crawls out onto the surface of the water to let its wings unfurl and dry at which point it is called a "Dun". After its wings are dry, the insect flies away to the streamside foliage where it stays for about two weeks while undergoing a second metamorphoses. After fully maturing, the Dun molts and emerges from its exoskeleton again as a sexually mature adult which is called a "Spinner".

Caddis fly imitations, on the other hand, are many fly angler's favorite dry fly pattern and they are designed to imitate an adult

Caddis fly that is returning to the water to lay its eggs. Looking a little deeper into the life cycle of the Caddis fly we see that Caddis flies are born as eggs laid on the streambed that then hatch into larvae of two different types depending on species. After hatching, some larva build a cocoon to which they attach small pebbles or sticks and leaves (aka "pebble bait" and "stick bait" respectively) while other species live as free roaming, predatory, larva. However, when both types of larva are ready to hatch, those that don't already have cocoons build them and then both types seal themselves in like a caterpillar and then undergo a metamorphoses into a sexually mature adult. Once the metamorphosis is complete, the adult exits the cocoon, quickly rises to the surface, and then exits the water immediately.

Consequently, all dry fly patterns are intended to be fished on the surface and allowed to float along with the current but, it is absolutely imperative that they be drifted drag free in order to appear as natural insects to the trout. Otherwise, they will be ignored.

Wet Flies -

Wet fly patterns are designed to be fished sub-surface in the top or middle of the water column and are designed to imitate adult May Fly duns that have either drowned while floating on the surface of the stream waiting for their wings to dry or died while flying over the water after laying their eggs. In addition, they differ from dry flies in that they are made from soft hackle material instead of stiff hackle material and their wings are swept to the rear instead of standing upright. However, they too must be drifted drag free in order to appear as natural insects to the trout.

Emergers -

Emerger patterns are fished in the surface film and are designed to represent a Mayfly nymph that has risen to the surface and is suspended in the surface film while it splits its carapace to emerge as a Dun.

Terrestrials -

Terrestrials are a sub-category of dry flies and thus they are fished on the surface like a dry fly. Also, Terrestrial fly patterns are designed to imitate insects that live on the ground or in the trees along the side of a stream which have accidentally fallen into the water or been blown into the water by the wind. Thus, terrestrial patterns such as beetles, ants, and inchworms, ect. make excellent search patterns for the late spring through late fall months.

Streamers -

Streamer patterns are fished sub-surface near the middle or bottom of the water column and are designed to imitate small baitfish that live in the stream such as Trout, Dace, Darters, and Sculpins.

Imitators -

Imitator patterns are what most people envision when they think of trout flies. However, they can be either dries, wets, or streamers that are tied to closely resemble actual species of aquatic insects, crustaceans, and forage fish. Thus, use imitators when fish are rising to insect hatches, when fish are finicky and refuse attractor patterns, and in calm, clear, water where fish have plenty of time to look at your fly before choosing to inhale it.

Attractors -

Attractor patterns are brightly colored dry fly, wet fly, and streamer patterns that don't resemble any actual insects or forage fish but still draw strikes nonetheless. However, biologists, fly tiers, and experienced fly fishermen all generally agree that there are some combinations of colors that automatically trigger the strike instinct in fish. For instance, trout are often triggered by the colors red, yellow, and green and a combination of red and white, yellow and white, and green and white while Smallmouth

Bass are often triggered by the colors olive green and chartreuse. Thus, attractor patterns are often useful for locating fish when there is no hatch coming off and/or the fish are not actively feeding. Also, attractor streamer patterns are often useful in turbid water because they are easier for the trout to see.

How to Read a Trout Stream -

Have you ever been out on a trout stream and noticed that some sections of the stream are narrow and swift while other sections are wide and slow? Well, as fly fishermen, we have names for these different types of water and they are Riffles, Runs, Pools, and Glides and, under normal circumstances, the laws of stream hydraulics dictates that these different sections occur in the order mentioned above. Thus, it is important for the fly fisherman to be able to identify each type of water and to understand where the trout are holding in each type of water as well as how to properly present a fly to the trout holding there. In addition, it is equally important that the fly angler be able to identify barren water versus productive water so that they do not waste their time drifting their flies over or through water where trout are not holding (although the particular locations where trout position themselves are called "trout lies", trout are said to "hold" there instead of "lie" there).

So, what constitutes barren water and what constitutes productive water? Well, first of all, barren water is any water that is to shallow to offer protection from avian predators or which has a bright, sandy, bottom that negates the Trout's camouflage and thus, outlines him to predators. Productive water on the other hand is water that is 12" deep or more, has a dark bottom, and is either directly in, or adjacent to, the main current.

Furthermore, different sections of the stream have distinctly different characteristics and thus, fly fishermen have chosen to give them descriptive names such a Riffles, Runs, Pools, and Glides. But, what is a Riffle, where do the trout hold in a Riffle, and where do you drift your fly in a Riffle in order to place it in front of the Trout? Well, a Riffle is a section of the stream where the current is fairly swift but, the water level is fairly shallow and it flows over a bed of small, round, rocks or pebbles. Thus, the entire surface of a Riffle consists of small wavelets and mild white water. Consequently, Riffles are the aerators of the trout stream and, because they hold the most dissolved oxygen of any section in the stream and, because they offer easy access to food, the entire riffle becomes a Prime lie if it is deep enough. Therefore, to fish a riffle, station yourself either downstream of or adjacent to it, while facing the riffle and then mentally divide the riffle into lanes about a foot wide. Then, cast your fly to the top of the first "lane" closest to you and let it drift for the entire length of the riffle (or as far as you can) and then, pick it up and recast it to the next lane over and let it drift. Then, you simply repeat this process until you have covered the entire riffle from side to side (called "fan casting"). Last, please note that it may sometimes be necessary to wade into the riffle in order to reach your next lane over which is fine as long as you do it SLOWLY. But, "what about the food vs. energy equation" you might ask? Well, Trout are anatomically designed in such a way that when holding in swift current against a flat bottom, all they have to do is place their lower jaw against the stream bed and the current with push them down and hold them there just like the wing on the rear end of a race car. Then, in order to obtain food, all they have to do is tilt their Pectoral fins just a bit and the current will cause them to rise or descend though the water column.

Next, what is a Run, where do the trout hold in a Run, and how do you fish a run? Well, a run is a section of the stream where the current becomes very narrow, very swift, and is usually quite deep (although not always). Thus, because the current is much swifter in a Run than it is in a Riffle, the Prime Lies in a Run are *adjacent* to the current rather than in it. Therefore, look for large rocks either above or below the surface of the water as well as undercut ledges that will create eddies that provide the trout with shelter from the current but easy access to any aquatic insects drifting in the current. Then, drift your fly in the current as close to those Prime Lies as possible so that the trout has the least amount of distance to cover in order to seize your fly. In addition, Runs often extend into a Pool below them and thus, you will see a tongue of very swift water that extends into a body of much calmer water. Therefore, the edges of this current tongue are also Prime Lies and thus, you should cast your fly to the top of the current tongue right along the edge of seam between the swift water and the calm water and let it drift the entire length of current tongue.

Now, how do we define a Pool, where do the Trout hold in a Pool, and how do we present our fly to them? Well, a pool is defined as a small to large section of the stream that has a flat, calm, surface. Also, be aware that pools can be either very shallow, very deep, or anywhere in between but, they all have a (relatively) calm, smooth, surface. Consequently, this makes it much easier for predators to spot Trout in pools and thus, Trout have evolved super effective camouflage to prevent them from being detected when they are holding in calm water. However, if you take a dark colored object and place it over a light colored background, the dark object is immediately obvious because it is outlined by the light background and the same thing happens to trout when they swim over a bright, sandy, bottom in a Pool. Therefore, the Prime Lies in a Pool are going to be at the head of the Pool where any aquatic insects drifting with the current will first enter the Pool and along the edges of the current tongue that extends into the pool from the Run or waterfall above it. However, if it is a large pool, there may be other places where the trout are holding such as any area with a dark bottom or a shadow from an overhanging tree (especially if it is strewn with varying sized rocks), behind or beneath logs that either extend into the stream from the bank or are submerged and are laying on the streambed, and along the banks under overhanging trees as long as there is enough current there to deliver a steady flow of aquatic insects.

Last, what is a Glide, where do we find the trout in a Glide, and how do we present our fly to them once we find them? Well, a Glide is essentially a Pool that is too long to be considered a proper Pool. For instance, picture in your mind your average, backyard, swimming pool and then, picture that same pool ten or twelve times longer and you will have the idea of the difference between a Pool and a Glide. Consequently, Glides are the most difficult of all trout waters to fish because the surface is so calm and the water is usually deep enough that the trout have a fairly wide Cone of Vision and thus, they can see any angler coming from a long ways off. In addition, due to the calm current in Glide, the trout tend to cruise rather than hold (although this is not always true). Therefore, in order to fish a Glide, you will need a fast action rod with a light weight, floating, line and a long leader so that you can make long casts that will land gently on the water's surface and enable you to stay out of the Trout's Cone of

Vision. Furthermore, rather than fish the entire Glide blind, stay on the bank and use the intervening foliage to hide your presence as you slowly sneak upstream looking for cruising trout. Then, when you spot one, move back downstream beyond the trout's Cone of Vision before casting your fly to it.

Consequently, it is extremely important for all novice fly fishermen to become adept at reading the stream and learning to differentiate between barren water and productive water. Also, it is imperative that you learn to determine where the Prime Lies are in each type of water and how to present your fly effectively to any tout holding in those Prime Lies if you are to become a successful fly fisherman.

How to Approach a Trout Lie -

Once you have learned to identify feeding and prime lies within a stream, you will need to learn how to approach the lie without spooking the fish. Thus, it is helpful at this point to adopt the attitude of a hunter rather than that of a fisherman. First, you must understand that a trout grows up *paranoid* and rightly so because there a lot of predators that like to eat trout. Consequently, as mentioned previously, a trout's mentality is "If it moves, RUN! If it doesn't move, RUN ANYWAY!" In addition, it is important to remember that Trout have *330 degrees of horizontal vision and 160 degrees of vertical vision!* Thus, a trout lying beneath the surface of the water will have a cone of vision that is 2 ¼ times the water's depth through which they can see the surface world that grows smaller as the trout rises or as the water gets shallower (called Snell's Law). Furthermore, while it is not likely that trout have the ability to recognize us as humans, they do have thousands of years of genetic memory that tells them what a Bear looks like and, since a human looks vaguely like a bear standing on its hind legs, sight of a human automatically triggers their flight response. So, when approaching a trout in either Feeding Lies or Prime Lies, it is imperative that you stop and closely examine the lie you intend to fish and its surrounding area and then create a plan of approach to account for the type of terrain and water flow you will have to wade through to reach a viable casting position. Next, it is important to note, and take advantage of, any cover that you may use to conceal your approach such as streamside foliage, boulders and large rocks, logs, and/or sandbars. Then, once you have taken note of any streamside foliage that may interfere with your cast, any still water that may cause ripples, any rough terrain that may cause you to slip or stumble, and any cover you can use to conceal yourself, then you can plan your approach to the lie you intend to fish. But, because trout have 160° of vertical vision, that leaves a fly fisherman a mere 10° to hide in! So, whenever you are not concealed by cover of some sort, you *must* crouch down as low as possible to avoid being seen by the trout while moving into your chosen casting position. Then, once you are where you want to be, you must still remain as low to the water's surface as possible in order to avoid being seen by the trout while casting. Therefore, try practicing your cast in your yard while both kneeling and sitting.

Basic Short Range Fly Casting Technique -

In order to understand how to properly cast a fly, it is very important to first understand the basic mechanics involved in proper fly casting technique and to then instill those mechanics in your body by building "muscle memory".

Thus, you first need to understand that casting a fly is divided into two actions and each action is further divided into two motions. Consequently, the first action is called the "Back Cast" because you use this action to pick the fly line up off of the water and cast it behind you. Then, the second action is called the "Forward Cast" because this action is used to cast the fly line from behind you to in front of you and to aim the fly at your intended target. In addition, each of these casting actions is further divided into two separate motions which will be explain separately.

First of all, to perform the Back Cast, you need understand that it is divided into two motions that consist of a "lift" and a "power stroke". Furthermore, it is important to understand that the lifting motion is performed with the *forearm only* and with wrist locked in the forward position. Then, the "power stroke" is performed with the *wrist only* and with the forearm locked in position. Thus, to perform the back cast, you start with the tip of your fly rod as close to the water as possible without submerging it.

Then, you slowly lift the fly line off of the water and, once it has done so, you increase the speed of your forearm until your rod tip reaches a position approximately equal to 10:30 on a clock face.

Then, at this point, you stop moving your forearm and start moving *only your wrist*. Next, to perform the "power stroke" you move your wrist from the 10:30 position to the 1:00 o'clock position while applying force to the rod. However, it is *very important* to understand that at this point, you are attempting to cast the fly line high in the air behind you and thus it is *imperative* that you do not drop your rod tip lower than 1:00 o'clock!

Next, you will need to perform a Forward Cast to launch the fly line out in front of you toward your intended target. Therefore, you need understand that the Forward Cast is divided into two motions as well that consist of a "push" and a "power stroke". Also, as it is with the Back Cast, the Forward Cast is performed by first moving the *forearm only* and then by moving the *wrist only*. Thus, with your rod tip held at the 1:00 o'clock position and, with the fly line extended in the air behind you after completing your backcast, you need to hesitate a moment in order to allow your back cast to fully straighten out behind you (called "finishing your back cast") at which point you will feel a slight tug on the end of your fly rod which is your indicator that it is then time to start your forward cast.

Then, to perform the Forward Cast, you start by once again locking your wrist and moving *only your forearm*. However, when performing this motion, you need to move your forearm forward while causing your wrist to move **horizontally** *in a straight line* by "pushing" your forearm forward until your rod tip reaches the 12:00 o'clock position.

Then, at that point, you stop moving your forearm and start moving *only your wrist* to perform the "power stroke" until the rod tip reaches the 11:00 o'clock position in front of you.

Thus, the most common mistakes people make when performing the Back Cast is that they drop their rod tip past the 1:00 o'clock position to 2:00 o'clock or even 3:00 o'clock. So, even if you have heard the phrase "10 to 2" in reference to fly casting, *ignore* it because it's WRONG! In addition, people tend to start their Forward Cast too soon after performing their Back Cast and this often results in causing the end of the fly line to snap like a bull whip and can actually snap the fly off of the end of your fly line leader! In addition, when performing the Forward Cast, people tend to pivot their forearm around their elbow in an arc instead of moving their forearm forward in such a way that it pushes their wrist straight forward *horizontally*. Consequently, pivoting your forearm around your elbow will cause the tip of your fly rod to dive toward the surface of the water as you finish your forward cast and thus, it will drive your fly line straight down instead out into the air in front of you. Therefore, when performing the Forward Cast, it is helpful to use the tip of your fly rod to *aim* the fly line at your target but, most importantly, use the tip of your fly rod to aim the fly line *above* the water and not at the water's surface. The idea here being that you want your fly line to straighten out above the surface of the water and slowly float down to land on the water instead of slapping the water as it lands.

Last, the easiest way to instill these motions properly in your "muscle memory" to set your fly rod aside, cup the elbow of your casting arm with the palm of your other hand, and then *slowly* perform each movement and each action numerous times without the fly rod. This will teach you to keep your elbow in close to your body when casting which will make your casting motion far more efficient and it will allow your body to learn how to make each movement and each action properly. Then, once you have instilled these motions and actions into your "muscle memory", pick up your fly rod and practice until you are able to place the fly on target every time without the fly line snapping behind you or driving into the water in front of you.

So, by reading and absorbing the above listed information, you should have all of the basic knowledge that you need to enable you to choose an appropriate fly rod, fly reel, fly line, and fly leader as well as all of the accessories that you will need for a day on the stream. Also, you should now have a basic understanding of how to find places to fly fish, what a Trout's habitat is like, what types of flies to use to catch them, how to read a trout stream, how to approach a Tout's lie, and how to cast a fly to the Trout in those lies. However, you should also be aware that this is only the most basic information and thus, a far more intensive study should be undertaken as your skills and experience as a fly fisherman grow in order to better enable you to catch this most wary and wiley of fish species.

Made in the USA
Monee, IL
14 August 2022